PRAISE FOR AC

"May Busch brings decades experience and a passion for learn. _ ....
Accelerate. Highly energetic in its approach and desired outcomes for leaders, *Accelerate* gives readers **a high-powered battery charge for future change and success."** | **Michael M. Crow**, President, Arizona State University

"This book IS for you. The path, action plans, and experiential breadth apply wherever you might be in your work, your career, and, most importantly, your life." | **Craig Weatherup**, former CEO of Pepsi-Cola

"Accelerate is **a must-read for any professional looking to achieve career mastery.** May provides real-life examples and 9 principles--with action plans--to avoid the mistakes, emulate the steps to her success, and accelerate your career." | **Leonard Kim**, *Inc.* magazine columnist, brand strategist, and managing partner at Influence Tree

"Insightful, practical, and full of valuable advice, May Busch's *Accelerate* is a contemporary guide for achieving career success today with essential steps and tools for managing your people, your business, and your self." | **Herminia Ibarra**, The Cora Chaired Professor of Leadership and Learning, INSEAD, and author of *Act Like a Leader, Think Like a Leader*

"Whether your career approach needs just a few tiny pivots or a complete overhaul, *Accelerate* will show you how to bridge the gap between your potential and your achievements. **Inspiring and practical at the same time!"** | **Marshall Goldsmith**, #1 *New York Times*–bestselling author of *Triggers, MOJO,* and *What Got You Here Won't Get You There*

Accelerate

9 Capabilities to Achieve Success at Any Career Stage
By May Busch

Old Avenue Press

Published by Old Avenue Press, London, United Kingdom
Copyright ©2016 May Busch
All rights reserved.

Copyeditor: Lisa Canfield, www.copycoachlisa.com
Index: Elena Gwynn, www.quillandinkindexing.com
Cover and Interior design: Yvonne Parks, www.pearcreative.ca
Cover copy: Lisa Canfield, www.copycoachlisa.com

ISBN: 978-0-9935451-0-8

ACCELERATE

9 CAPABILITIES
TO ACHIEVE SUCCESS
AT ANY CAREER STAGE

MAY BUSCH

CONTENTS

INTRODUCTION

YOUR GUIDE TO AN ACCELERATED PATH TO SUCCESS

If you're reading this book, then I'm guessing you're someone who values achievement, excellence and success—whether for yourself or others who matter to you—and that you want to be better, do more, and make the difference you were meant to make in the world.

You strive to bring your A-Game to work every day so you can make a unique contribution and be valued for it. You seek to live your values while moving up in the organization, and prove that "nice guys" can finish first. You want to have enough money in the bank so you can retire early and be free to do whatever you want.

And then you arrive at the office, get pulled in a hundred directions, and it's not so easy to accomplish these bigger goals.

Having walked more than the proverbial mile in those shoes, I know that sometimes it feels like tough going, that the "good guys" don't win, and that maybe it just isn't worth it. All I can say is: take heart. You are not alone, you *can* win, and we want—even need—you to keep going!

In fact, there were lots of painful moments during my 24-year investment banking career, whether it was seeing others get promoted ahead of me, making the wrong hiring decision, being reorganized out of a job, or upsetting my boss in a big way. And that's just to name a few. In those painful times, I learned the most. And despite those missteps and mistakes, I ended up achieving my goal of becoming a Managing Director and, ultimately, Chief Operating Officer for Europe.

If I can do it, you can too. And the good news is that I took good notes along the way. So now that I'm in my second career as a coach, speaker, and writer, I'm going to share what I know with you, so you and other achievers can succeed faster, with less pain and with greater ease.

This support is more important than ever because the world of work is more complex, more pressured, and faster-paced than ever before. Based on my work with executive-level and aspiring leaders, I see how hard it is for even the smartest, most capable people to remain focused on the bigger picture of their goals, both for their organization and for their career.

Everyone, at every level, is "doing more with less" support. The technology at our disposal means we're more interconnected and always on. We're maxed out on redoubling our efforts. As a result, it often feels like there's no time to think.

Many people describe the sensation of running hard just to stay still. If this sounds like you, some days, it might even feel like you're about to fall off the back of the treadmill.

As a result of, or parallel to, this personal anxiety, there's often a low-grade organizational anxiety (similar to a low-grade fever) that is simmering in many teams and companies. It's a feeling that's not only hard to shake, but that is also a drain on everyone's energy. This organizational anxiety—"Are we making budget?" "Is another re-org being planned that no one is telling us about?" "Is someone going to eat our lunch?"—keeps the collective on edge. On an individual level, it can sap your focus and confidence and keep you from being at your best.

On top of it all, instead of feeling like you're part of a team all pulling together, you can feel secretly alone. It's a reality that both mid-level and senior managers have less time to mentor others and guide talented people through the organization. In some cases, they're also less inclined to pull others up based on fear for the security of their own positions.

So, if you're feeling confused about where you are in your career, how well you're really doing, what could be next—whether that's with your current organization or somewhere else, know that your reactions are perfectly natural, and that many others feel the same way. In fact, some of them have overcome these feelings to go on to win and keep winning big in their careers and life. Why not you, too?

You can develop a strategy that gets you where you want to go—your own Achiever Path. That's what this short book is designed to do: to help you assess and act on the What, Where, When and How of advancing your career so you can fulfill your potential and make the difference you are meant to make.

So how do you do that? Well, there are three overarching tasks that make up the Achiever Path:

1. **Develop your Capabilities** beyond the technical skills needed to do your job.

2. **Own your own development** including a bigger picture view of the path ahead.

3. **Be prepared for big and small milestones** so you can master the "gates" along the path.

DEVELOP YOUR CAPABILITIES—THE THREE DIMENSIONS OF CAREER ACHIEVEMENT

Over the years, through my own career and now through helping my coaching clients navigate their leadership and career challenges, I've come to see that technical skills alone are not enough to advance to senior levels.

So, when I talk about "Capabilities," I'm looking beyond the skills you need to perform specific tasks such as preparing a legal brief, analyzing the financials, or creating the perfect presentation materials for a client pitch.

Looking beyond technical excellence, there are three main dimensions of ability where you need to demonstrate mastery in order to position yourself for the role and level you're aspiring to:

1. **Working with People.** The way you interact with others matters since none of us succeeds on our own.

2. **Working on the Business.** The ability to deliver results matters whether you're in a business, non-profit, higher education or government setting.

3. **Working on Your Self.** Understanding yourself and being able to bring out your best regardless of the situation provides the foundation for your success in your career and life.

Across these categories, I find it useful to focus on nine main Capabilities—three in each dimension—that can make the biggest difference in whether you "arrive" and achieve your definition of success or not.

3 DIMENSIONS OF CAREER ACHIEVEMENT

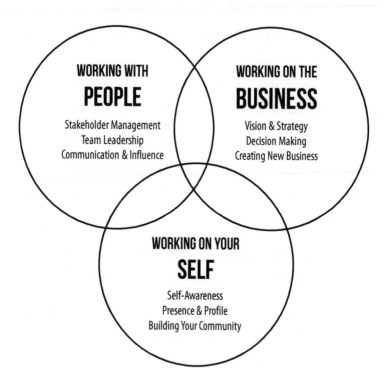

WORKING WITH
PEOPLE

Stakeholder Management
Team Leadership
Communication & Influence

WORKING ON THE
BUSINESS

Vision & Strategy
Decision Making
Creating New Business

WORKING ON YOUR
SELF

Self-Awareness
Presence & Profile
Building Your Community

Before we move on to the specifics of the 9 Capabilities, it's important to note that these three dimensions (Working with People, Working on the Business, and Working on Your Self) are all equally important. You'll want to make sure you're building your career muscles in all three.

While one of the categories will come more naturally to you than others, don't fall into the trap of becoming lopsided in your approach.

Being over-reliant on just one or two aspects has stopped many achievers from advancing beyond a certain point in their careers. Don't let that be you!

OWN YOUR OWN DEVELOPMENT—THE S-CURVE OF YOUR CAREER PATH

Unless you lead a truly charmed life where your desires are anticipated and handed to you on a platter, we all get to a point in our careers when we realize we have to take ownership if we want to achieve our career goals. Career success doesn't just happen.

For most of the people I've mentored and coached over the years, this realization has tended to occur when they are dissatisfied with their careers—usually somewhere in mid-career. But the sooner you understand this, the better off you will be.

Whenever you get to that point, it's helpful to be able to visualize your entire career at a strategic level, and here's the best way I've found to do it:

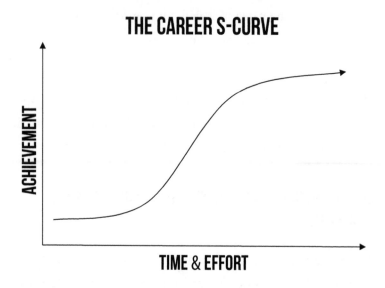

THE CAREER S-CURVE

(Chart: vertical axis labeled ACHIEVEMENT, horizontal axis labeled TIME & EFFORT, showing an S-shaped curve)

Think of the S-Curve as representing your career potential. It also serves as a map—like those floor plan directories in shopping malls with a big orange dot marked, "You are here."

Just as with the shopping mall map, the two most important questions for your career map are: (1) Where are you now? and (2) Where are you going (i.e., what does "success" look like for you)? Being able to clearly identify those two points makes it much easier to navigate from here to there.

Within the S-Curve, let's think of your career in three primary stages:

1. **Aspiring.** The early stage

2. **Driving.** The middle stage

3. **Arriving.** The advanced stage

THREE CAREER STAGES

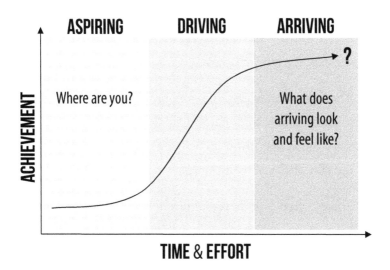

1. **Aspiring**. When you're just starting out and exploring options. You're working really hard, developing skills and gaining a variety of experiences. But your visible achievement is still quite modest because you're building a foundation.

2. **Driving.** When you've chosen where you want to make your mark and have to demonstrate all the things that it takes to be excellent in your chosen field. In my case, it was how to run a deal, lead a team, build client relationships, and become a "rainmaker."

3. **Arriving.** When you've achieved the level of success that you wanted—or had your sights set on. You're still working

hard but you've achieved so much that the incremental achievements no longer seem as big. This is because expectations have risen along with your capabilities, and here I mean your own expectations for yourself as well as the expectations of others.

4. **The Question Mark.** At some point during this Arriving stage, you may find yourself thinking, "What's next?" "Is this all there is?" And indeed, there is a question mark at the end of the Arriving stage.

That's when you have some choices to make. Do you keep doing what you've been doing and "coast" a bit? Do you decide to get on a new S-Curve, whether that's re-upping your commitment to advance where you are or doing something completely different? If you're at a later or senior stage of your career, do you opt out and retire altogether or take a sabbatical?

The good news is that none of us are limited to just one S-Curve in our careers. In fact, your overall career S-Curve is made up of smaller S-Curves that link up. While each distinct segment of your career constitutes a different S-Curve, you don't have to start all the way at the bottom when you jump onto a new S-Curve. That's because you've developed skills, capabilities, experience and wisdom along the way that you can build on.

For example, my first career S-Curve—from Analyst to Associate to Vice President and ultimately Managing Director and then COO—was my 24-year investment banking career. I then got to the question mark and chose to get on a new S-Curve and become an entrepreneur who helps achievers accelerate their journey to success. In my second S-Curve, I'm in the Driving stage.

BE PREPARED FOR BIG AND SMALL MILESTONES—MASTERING HIDDEN CAREER GATES

Along the S-Curve are milestones where you have to demonstrate you've got what it takes to advance: that "right mix" of competencies and attributes crucial to winning the support of key people in your career. I call these "Career Gates," because the situation reminds me of steeplechase races where the horse and rider have to jump over gates in a particular order and are judged by how well they do this. If they crash into a gate or miss it entirely, the judges penalize them. The same goes in our careers. But unlike steeplechase, it's often unclear what the gates are and we're left to figure it out for ourselves.

These Gates or key rites of passage will look different at different points along the career S-Curve, and are surprisingly powerful in determining whether you move forward, get stuck, or even derail.

Sometimes, my clients find it easier to see the Career Gates they've experienced in the past. I often see the light bulbs go off when they think back on why they didn't get a particular promotion, or why someone else was chosen to lead that big project. For some, they see that they needed to work on being better with people, or some other Capability. For others, they realize they had the "right mix" but didn't demonstrate it to the right people—that is, the decision-makers.

Where it gets really interesting is when my clients start anticipating the Career Gates that are likely to come up next. For Charlotte, it was the lead-up to the next promotion and needing to demonstrate that she could manage her stakeholders, get people on board with her strategy and act with confidence. For Dan, it was winning over a new department head who was looking for leaders who could create new business lines and build up the team.

In an ideal world, we would all sail through our Career Gates by demonstrating to the right people that we've got what it takes when it matters. We would all have perfect careers! Yet, in my own case and through my work with talented achievers, I've discovered that it's all too easy to miss Career Gates, in which case career progress can slow or even plateau without our realizing it. Yes, even when we're eminently qualified and work harder than everyone else.

Sometimes, my smartest clients have the biggest blind spots. This is what holds them back from passing through Career

Gates, especially during the Driving stage. Often, it's because they don't realize that key people are forming impressions of them in the normal course of business, not just when it's a formal situation.

In essence, we're auditioning for our part every day without realizing it. That's why it pays to be prepared.

CAREER GATES

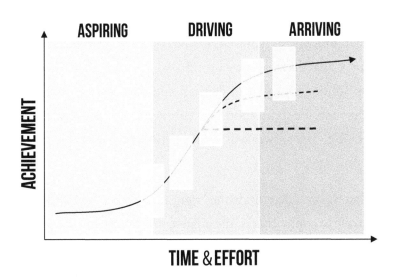

As an aside, it's fine to plateau in your career if you do so intentionally, whether to take time out for family, personal or other priorities. But it's really a shame to see achievers plateau when they don't intend to. That's what this awareness and practice of the Capabilities can offer you. There are specific actions and steps you can take to develop, enhance, and publicly "show your stuff" without "playing politics" and this will serve to advance you as well as your team.

Once you can recognize and anticipate Career Gates, you can start turning them into opportunities rather than obstacles. Otherwise, you're leaving things to chance—and as they say, "hope is not a strategy."

FOCUS ON THE CAPABILITIES THAT MATTER MOST RIGHT NOW

Of course, in our already overstressed work environments, you'll overwhelm yourself if you imagine working on *all* your Capabilities all at once. So what's the "right mix" of Capabilities you need to develop and demonstrate to others right now? Keep in mind that this is not a "once and done" question. The answer will continually change over the course of your career.

Whatever you determine the "right mix" to be, the 80/20 rule is likely to apply. That is, the biggest step change in your results (i.e., the 80%) will be driven by improvements you make in a small subset of capabilities (i.e., the 20%). So instead of working on nine things at the same time, identify the one or two Capabilities that could make the biggest difference to your progress if you were to focus on them right now.

You may know intuitively what they are, or perhaps you've been told in your latest performance review. If you don't know, then asking a few people you trust will help reveal them.

Here are a few questions that can help you get input:

- What do you see as my biggest strength in our work context?

- If you were to advise me on the one thing I could work on that would make the biggest difference in my ability to add value right now, what would that be?

- Looking ahead, what's the one thing that could hold me back in the future if I don't start developing it now?

Now, take a look at the Capabilities on pages 16 & 17 and identify which ones are your strongest, your most challenging, and the single most important one for you to work on right now to advance your career.

By the way, the single most important Capability to work on is the one that gives you the biggest boost—which may not be the area that's weakest or most challenging for you. It may even be a strength that you need to lean into. It's the one capability that will most move the needle for you now and in the future. Where do you get the greatest benefit from investing your energy to improve?

9 ACHIEVER CAPABILITIES

WORKING WITH PEOPLE

1. **Stakeholder Management**. Building relationships with key people who have a say in your business in order to get the backing you need without being "political."

2. **Team Leadership**. Becoming a great leader who is a talent magnet and builds a strong bench of leaders around you so that you can achieve greater results and make a positive difference in the organization and in the lives of your team.

3. **Communication and Influence**. Being clear, engaging, and effective in getting your point across, and having the versatility to influence people in different situations and in different ways so that you can get things done when you lack or want to preserve authority.

WORKING ON THE BUSINESS

4. **Vision and Strategy**. Developing a bigger vision for what your business could be beyond what it is now, and having a strategy for owning that "space" so that you can produce better results and earn a seat at the table with senior management.

5. **Decision Making**. Preserving your decision making capacity so you can crisply make the ones that really

count and learning to frame the key decisions to get to the best outcomes so that you can be seen as a decisive leader with good judgment who is worthy of advancement.

6. **Creating New Business.** Being a "rainmaker" who delivers commercial results and grows the pie— regardless of where you sit in the organization—so that you can contribute to driving the business forward and earn greater opportunities for advancement and recognition for you and your team.

WORKING ON YOUR SELF

7. **Self-Awareness.** Being attuned to how you come across and able to self-manage in order to achieve the results you want.

8. **Presence and Profile.** Managing your brand, reputation and visibility so that you increase the likelihood of getting opportunities to put your best abilities to work in arenas where you can make a difference, advancing your business and your career, and providing greater opportunities for your team.

9. **Building Your Community.** Creating a group of people where there is mutual trust, respect, and support, including mentors, sponsors, and raving fans, so that you can be in a position to be your best self and make the difference you a were meant to make in the world.

Working on these 9 Achiever Capabilities will put you in a much better position to pass through your Career Gates whether or not you're aware they're there. In the pages that follow, we will explore each of the 9 Capabilities including:

- Highlights of the Capability

- How it looks when done well or poorly

- What can go wrong

- Specific, action-oriented suggestions to help you increase your effectiveness in this arena

The final chapter lays out a simple, self-guided path to help you summarize and capture your key takeaways so that you can take action and accelerate your career progress.

As you explore your career and your Achiever Capabilities, avoid thinking of them like assignments or school papers that you turn in and never look at again—these are living, breathing Capabilities that you need to keep fresh and evolve based on your growing maturity, the changing dynamics and goals of your organization, and the aspects of your career that are most exciting, creative, and rewarding for you. The more actively you engage with this work—and even think of it as "play"—the more success and ease you'll enjoy.

You'll want to return to the Capabilities over and over again to continue your development in increasingly advanced and nuanced ways, because they will help you keep progressing to higher levels of excellence as your career progresses.

Remember, start with the one or two Capabilities that will most move the needle for you right now, and focus on those. The more you work on them, the better you'll become and the more natural they will be. Then you'll be on your way to creating a virtuous cycle that can lift your career onward and upward.

In the words of a recent client who was even more encouraged about her career prospects after starting to take action, "It's fun when things pan out!"

And now, it's time for you to jump in so you can have more fun and success with your career too.

WORKING WITH PEOPLE

Today's uncertain, volatile and fast-moving environment means that our ability to work with and relate to people is more important to our success than ever before.

Working with People includes three specific Capabilities:

1. **Stakeholder Management.** Being able to build relationships with the key people who have a say in what and how you do your work, whether or not you like each other.

2. **Team Leadership.** Building and maintaining a high performing team in order to deliver bigger results.

3. **Communication & Influence.** Communicating effectively with a wide range of people in a way that allows you to influence outcomes.

CHAPTER 1

STAKEHOLDER MANAGEMENT: BUILDING KEY RELATIONSHIPS

At the very start of your career, it can be enough to keep your head down, turn out excellent work, and do what your boss tells you to do. After all, at that point your boss is the main person determining your projects, pay, and promotion.

Once you get beyond the training program stage, it takes more than just impressing one person to get and stay ahead. In fact, the more senior you get, the more people you come in contact with, and the more people have a say in what you do and how well you do it. These people are your stakeholders.

For example, if the technology project you're leading affects the powerful sales and product development teams, then you're more likely to succeed if you've already built a trusted relationship with your counterparts in those groups, and bring them into the picture early on so they can help shape the solution instead of possibly vetoing it when it's sprung on them at the end.

At the mid-career level, your key stakeholders are still likely to be primarily internal, which includes your reporting line (boss, plus 1-2 levels up), immediate team members, and key colleagues in other product areas, geographical regions, support services areas, and functional areas (e.g., finance, legal, sales, operations, HR, marketing). External stakeholders would include any external clients you may have, and of course, your family.

By the time you get to the CEO, Senior Vice President, and division head levels, there's a broad range of internal and external stakeholders to manage, including the board, employees, customers, suppliers, the press, and regulators—just to name a few.

My client Charles excels at stakeholder management. Relative to his peers, he has a much easier time getting the best outcomes for his projects and his team. Charles knows and is known to his key stakeholders across the organization, which paves the way for projects and requests to move smoothly through the internal approval process. Those key people feel comfortable that they will not be "blind-sided" or surprised by what Charles and his team are doing.

That's because Charles has been keeping in touch with them regularly—an update email here and there, a quick fly-by hello as he's passing someone's office, an invitation to the department head to join a client meeting, a semi-annual coffee to get advice on his business strategy, and so forth. Through these actions, he has figured out the What, When, and How of keeping in touch with each individual in a way that's suited to their interests and needs, while being relatively easy for him. Having built these relationships, if something falls through the cracks, he has sufficient relationship chits to be able to recover and get back on track.

As an added benefit, when you master the Stakeholder Management Capability, you will have done 80-90% of the work to become adept at "navigating the politics," which is essential to your career success. And you will have done it without being political.

> When you manage your stakeholders well, you can create a virtuous cycle of accelerating the progress of your projects and the advancement of your career.

HOW EVEN THE SMARTEST PEOPLE CAN BLOW IT

Sam was a star on the investment bank's trading desk. He had gone to one of the "right schools." He was considered to be exceptionally bright at a firm of exceptionally bright people. Not only that, he had an uncanny sense for the markets he was responsible for. As a result, he was consistently the biggest producer on the desk and ultimately was put in charge of the unit.

Sam and his team saw themselves as a revenue-generating engine that didn't need the other divisions to accomplish their goals. In Sam's view, if other divisions ran their businesses the way he ran his, the shareholders would be better off. Sam aspired to be part of the firm's top management team one day.

However, at this higher managerial level, Sam needed to interact with the other areas of the firm directly, without his extremely diplomatic division head running interference.

Given his mindset, Sam soon developed a terrible reputation with the client relationship teams in other areas of the organization. They complained about his lack of regard for their interests as well as his refusal to engage in a constructive dialogue to resolve issues. No wonder—Sam thought they were dopes and wasn't interested in cooperating or collaborating. He was convinced they had nothing to add.

In the end, that was his downfall. Sam failed to understand that to get to the lofty positions he aspired to, he needed the support of people in those closed-door meetings where senior positions were determined. Even his previously supportive boss had to admit he could no longer push for Sam's advancement. And Sam ultimately left the firm.

How could such a brilliant intellect miss the point about needing to manage his stakeholder relationships? In retrospect, it seems that he didn't even recognize that they were stakeholders.

PUTTING STAKEHOLDER MANAGEMENT INTO PRACTICE

The more senior you become, the more important stakeholder management will be. Taking these four steps can help you improve those key relationships:

1. **Identify your stakeholders.** List out the top 5-10 people who have an interest in, are affected by, or can affect what you do and don't do. Whether internal or external to your organization, their buy-in is crucial to your success. If you don't know who they are, ask someone you trust who is politically savvy, and think about these categories:

⏻	People who can green light your project or kill it
⏭	People who can accelerate your progress
⏮	People who can set you back
🔇	People who can amplify what you do or recommend you to others
$	People who pay and promote you
★	People who recognize you for your performance

2. **Map them out**. Organize each according to their level of impact on your career (or business) and the strength of your relationship.

		RELATIONSHIP	
		WEAK	STRONG
IMPACT	HIGH	B	A
	LOW	D	C

Place your top 5-10 stakeholders into the relevant quadrant. You're in great shape with the As. You need to get to know the Bs. See if you can leverage your relationship with the Cs to help convert the Bs into As. The Ds are not a priority, unless they are likely to rise to become Bs.

3. **Put together a plan for the top 2-3 stakeholders on the list.** For each of those 2-3 stakeholders, write down their interests and what you can do to help them succeed, their concerns and how you can address them, and what you need to keep them apprised of and when.

4. **Take action.** To see how this Capability can work *for* you and not against you, you can start by completing the list. Then, pick a person from the A or B quadrants (or somewhere in between) for conversations in the next few weeks—someone where you have some confidence in connecting so you can "test" the value of creating, deepening, or repairing your stakeholder relationships.

PERSONAL ACTION PLAN
FOR STAKEHOLDER MANAGEMENT

Who are my 2-3 (or 3-5 max) main A and B stakeholders currently and what matters to them?

Who influences these stakeholders, and how well do we know each other?

Where do they "land" on the Relationship/Impact map? Are they an A, B, C, or D? (see page 28)

What steps can I take to build my relationship with those top 3-5 stakeholders and influencers?

I commit to take this one action each week to build my key stakeholder relationships:

CHAPTER 2

TEAM LEADERSHIP: BUILDING AND MAINTAINING A HIGH-PERFORMING TEAM

Most of us start our careers as individual contributors. We learn technical skills and develop expertise in a subject or function, such as legal expertise, financial analysis, copy writing, sales or conducting scientific experiments. Our clients and bosses look to us for our technical, subject matter, or functional expertise. Usually, this doesn't center on managing people.

However, there comes a point when all of us, even individual contributors, are expected to be able to lead a team if we are to advance. Perhaps a small team, but a team nonetheless. And to advance even further, including in a technical field, means being a leader of other individual contributors—in essence, a leader of people.

Making the shift from being an individual contributor to a team leader or unit leader is essential to advancing beyond mid-level. It's also one of the trickiest moves in a career. It means letting go of being known primarily for your technical expertise and learning to achieve greater outcomes through others than you could on your own. It's a fundamental mindset shift that people don't generally tell you how to make.

At the heart of team leadership is being able to build and maintain a high-performing team. That requires you to do three things:

1. **Bring out the best in the team**. That means taking a genuine interest in your people, as well as understanding what motivates them, their strengths and their development areas. That knowledge will help you delegate appropriately, inspire the team, and provide feedback in the most energizing way. Become a role model for the behavior you expect, and frame part of your role as building the next generation of leaders beneath you.

2. **Keep out the worst in yourself**. Don't be a "nightmare boss." While it may sound like setting our sights too low, my experience is that if a boss simply gets rid of his or her dysfunctions (and we all have them, whether it's micromanaging, avoiding confrontation, being too

confrontational, taking credit for others' work, etc.), it's enough to unleash substantial productivity and creativity from the team.

3. **Become a talent magnet.** Be someone people want to work for. When your group is known as a great place for people to make their careers and make a difference, the best and brightest will come to you. And you can then make the assessment of which people are the best fit.

Whatever your innate level of talent for leading teams, this is a Capability you can always improve and it's a Capability worth building because it will serve you well no matter what you do in your career.

> Beyond a certain point, your advancement will rely on your ability to lead people to collaborate and deliver greater value than the sum of their individual parts.

WHEN LEADERS CONTRIBUTE TOO MUCH

Paul is practically perfect in every way. He does his work to exceptionally high standards, has a huge work capacity, and frankly, does everything well. Not only that, he never complains about the gaps he has in staffing, and gratefully accepts the junior-level staff he's been given. Paul is the greatest thing since sliced bread … or is he?

That served Paul well for a while—a couple of years, even. However, here's the new reality as he gets more senior:

While Paul takes the juniors he's been given, they're not the best of the bunch, so when he delegates to them, he has to fix their work. That compounds the problem he faces from understaffing, which puts him at his limit for "doing more with less." The net effect is that he doesn't attract the best people because he tolerates mediocrity. This leaves Paul without a credible bench. He has no one to take over his role so he can't get promoted.

Meanwhile, his boss is looking at him and wondering why he's in every meeting on his own. Where is Paul's team? She doesn't see a bench below Paul at a time when he should be creating the next generation of leaders. While his output is still excellent, it doesn't seem to be sustainable. She's afraid he'll burn out.

Her admiration from the early days has turned into concern that there's a real issue going forward. But, is it the caliber of the team, Paul's inability to delegate and hold people accountable, or his failure to spend enough time developing his people? Or a mixture of all three?

Regardless of the answer, none of these explanations are positive for Paul's career.

PUTTING TEAM LEADERSHIP INTO PRACTICE

As the leader of the team, it's your job to set up the conditions for everyone to succeed. Here are five ways to do that:

BRING OUT THE BEST IN YOUR TEAM

1. **Let them know where they stand with you.** When you keep people wondering, you drain their energy through worrying when they could be pulling toward the common goal. Instead, get permission from your team members to give them feedback regularly and in real time. That way, it's normal and not such a big deal to have even tough conversations—just keep it constructive, and say it "with love and grace." You know how disheartening it can be to get to year-end and learn that you could have done things differently, by which time it's too late.

2. **Invest in your people.** Help them to become leaders themselves, which will make your job easier and allow you to step up sooner. Make sure they get to the training sessions they've signed up for. Use "teachable moments"—those unplanned-for situations where you can share your own knowledge and experience with them in real time.

3. **Don't be a bad boss.** Catch yourself if you find you're behaving like those people we all hate to work for, including (but not limited to!):

- **The Micromanager.** Delegates, but not really.

- **The Dr. Jekyll and Mr. Hyde.** You never know how they will react.

- **The Credit Stealer.** Takes credit for your great ideas.

- **The Public Berater.** Cuts you down in public, when a quiet word later would do.

- **The Sphinx.** Never provides any feedback or teaches you anything.

- **The "Too Nice" Boss.** Is a pushover, but secretly resents things... and you wonder whether he or she will stand up for you when it counts.

- **The Disorganized Boss.** Keeps you from getting things done and drops assignments on your desk at 5pm on Fridays.

4. **Make your group attractive.** Gain the reputation for being someone great to work for in a group that's going places. That means having an energizing vision and mission for the team as well as looking after the team members so that they can focus on doing their best work. When you're able to attract more interest than you have seats, recruiting is far easier. You'll have a choice of people rather than having to settle for second best.

5. **Choose well.** Focus on choosing the right people for the right roles, because there needs to be a match in order for your team to deliver superior results. Resist the natural instinct to hire in your own likeness—that is, avoid the "mini-me" trap. And don't hire "like-minded people." When everyone has the same views, the same background, and the same way of thinking, you get "groupthink," which ultimately leads to bad decisions and poor performance. It's far better to have a variety of voices and viewpoints around the table to keep the group robust, innovative, and heading in the right direction.

PERSONAL ACTION PLAN FOR TEAM LEADERSHIP

What specific behaviors and habits make me a great person to work for? How can I build on that?

What specific behaviors and habits make me difficult to work for? Are they serving me well?

Who's on my team and how can I help them develop and grow?

How can we become a group that people want to work for?

I commit to take this one action every day in order to become a better team leader:

CHAPTER 3

COMMUNICATION THAT CONNECTS: GETTING YOUR POINT ACROSS AND INFLUENCING OTHERS

Good communicators are clear, engaging, and effective in getting their point across in a way that others understand, whether in person or in writing. They also focus on understanding what others are communicating so there's mutual understanding on a consistent basis.

When you can communicate in a way that forms that kind of connection with others, you have a greater ability to influence outcomes and reach the goals you and your team are working toward.

Being a great communicator is a "linchpin" Capability. It has a knock-on effect on many other Achiever Capabilities. I like to think of being a great communicator as a "Super Food" that boosts your entire system by helping you:

- Build relationships and influence at every level—with clients, your boss, colleagues and juniors.

- Create buy-in for the initiatives you lead.

- Negotiate effectively for what you want and need.

In short, communicating effectively is a crucial aspect of your success whenever you're working with and for other people, which is most the time.

In my experience with both clients and colleagues, those who have excelled at communicating in a way that connects with people and influences outcomes do three things that others do not:

1. **They focus keenly on their audience.** They treat communication as a two-way street, not a one-way megaphone, and flex their style to suit the situation.

2. **They listen with an open mind.** They aren't simply waiting for an opening to restate their case more eloquently or to hammer on their points again.

3. **They understand and draw on their sources of influence.** Whether that's based on thought leadership,

expertise, passion, resources, connections, financial clout, or something else, it is part of their narrative.

Keep in mind that even the greatest communicators can still improve. So think progress, not perfection, and keep practicing your craft.

> "I've learned that people will forget what you said, people will forget what you did, but people will never forget how you made them feel." — Maya Angelou

THE POWER OF FEELING SEEN, HEARD, AND RESPECTED

When I was being recruited to return to Morgan Stanley after getting my MBA, I had the privilege of an audience with Dick Fisher, who was at that time the President of the firm.

Even though this was a "selling interview"—the firm selling me on them, not me selling myself (I already had my offer to return as an Associate)—I was nervous going up the elevator to the executive floor. I stepped out onto the thick carpet and an assistant walked me past the mahogany furniture and oil paintings toward Dick's office.

Dick greeted me at the door, shook my hand, and asked me to come in. We sat in two chairs quite close together on the Persian rug. While I'm sure there was not a fireplace on the 52nd floor of 1251 Avenue of the Americas, I will always remember this as a "fireside chat."

He asked me to tell him about myself, my interests, and how he could help me make this decision. He answered all my questions thoughtfully. When he finally asked if there was anything else I wanted to ask or discuss, I realized that I had had every question and concern addressed, and I felt that he understood me. I was ready to go.

Stepping back into the corridor, I felt amazed that he had spent so much time with me—it felt like we had talked for hours. But when I looked at my watch, I saw that only 20 minutes had passed! I signed up that afternoon.

This was one of the most amazing one-on-one communications I have ever experienced in a work context. I had never felt so completely listened to and by such a senior person who clearly would have had far more pressing matters than recruiting a new Associate to join the firm. He never looked at his watch or his phone—not even once. It was as though I was the only other person in the entire world.

What made Dick Fisher a powerful communicator was his ability to connect with people and make them feel respected and heard. And that is a powerful source of influence.

PUTTING COMMUNICATION AND INFLUENCE INTO PRACTICE

Whatever your mode of communication, there are some common principles you can adopt to be effective. Here are three steps to help you create mutual understanding:

1. **Understand the audience.** Great communication is like throwing a ball to another person. As the one doing the throwing, you're responsible for making sure the ball is thrown in a way that the other person can catch it.

   That means being audience centric. Tailor your message and adapt your style based on who they are and where they are coming from. Recognize that your audience will be listening with a WIIFM (What's In It For Me?) mindset. When you start with this in mind, you're more likely to engage, connect and influence.

2. **Prepare and deliver the core message.** Here are four ways to do it:

   - **Define success.** Identify the 2-3 things you want to achieve before you leave the room or end the conversation. That way, you're more likely to achieve your goal and also to know when to "stop talking once you've made the sale", because one word too many can ruin the entire conversation.

   - **The 5-minute rule.** Set aside 5 minutes before you go into the meeting, call, or conversation to step back from the detail, clear your mind of competing issues, stresses, and deadlines, and remind yourself of the primary message(s) you want to convey. That way you'll be more certain of achieving your objectives for the session.

- **The Rule of 3.** A proven way to package your message is to synthesize your ideas into three main points. Research shows that the human brain cannot absorb more than three ideas at a time, so it's no wonder the global consulting firm McKinsey adopts this rule.

- **Get to the point.** The more senior your audience, the more important it is to get straight to the point, and even start with the conclusion. If they want supporting points, they'll ask. Don't think that it's exciting to build up to a conclusion by starting with the details. Senior people don't have the time or patience to "wait for it …"

3. **Create a feedback loop.** Even the most eloquently delivered message is ineffective if it doesn't land in the way you intend. That's why it's key to ask questions, watch body language, listen for responses and check in to make sure they heard and received what you said.

- **Watch for the non-verbal cues.** What's not said can be as important as what is said. Are they crossing their arms? Frowning? Avoiding eye contact? These are clues and cues you can use to modify your approach in mid-stream.

- **Listen to with an open mind—not one that's wedded to your own position.** That's what it means to engage in "listening to understand." *Ask* a question that allows you to check your understanding, or play back what you heard.

PERSONAL ACTION PLAN
FOR COMMUNICATION THAT COUNTS

What are my main communication opportunities during the week? Where am I strong and where could I improve with more planning and effort?

For 1-2 opportunities that require more thought and planning, who is the audience and what outcomes do I want to achieve in communicating with them?

What is the mindset and WIIFM ("What's In It For Me?") of those audiences? How can this help me communicate my message in a way that "lands?"

What specific action, habit or attitude shift could I make to become a more engaging and powerful communicator?

I commit to take this one action every day in order to become a better communicator:

WORKING ON THE BUSINESS

These days, to be considered "high potential" requires being a "Game Changer"— someone who can close the opportunity gap between where we are now and where we *could* be. Now, that's a tall order because it involves leading both change and innovation at the same time. It's a challenge where there's no road map.

Being a Game Changer involves being able to envision the future of your business and devise a way to achieve that future (**Vision and Strategy**), make crisp decisions and put them into action (**Decision Making**), and deliver results that improve and expand the organization's horizons (**Creating New Business**).

CHAPTER 4

VISION AND STRATEGY: RECOGNIZING OPPORTUNITIES AND CHARTING NEW DIRECTIONS

Somewhere in the middle of your career, being good at vision and strategic thinking becomes an essential Capability. No one will ring a bell to alert you, but it's as if there is a big sifter that sorts the haves from the have-nots, and promotes the former at the expense of the latter.

Professor Herminia Ibarra's research refers to this Capability as "envisioning": the ability to recognize new opportunities and trends in the environment and develop a new strategic direction for an enterprise.

In my experience, there are three additional aspects to envisioning which include being able to:

1. Recognize how your own role (and that of your group) could evolve and contribute to the enterprise's future direction.

2. Articulate this future direction to others (your team, colleagues, recruits, mentors, etc.) in a way that is powerful and energizing.

3. Take a more strategic approach to the way you do your current work.

Think of *vision* as your aspiration for your business and your self—see what you could be in the future and what it would look like to win. Think of *strategy* as the way in which you're going to get from here to there—the high level game plan for winning.

For example, when we started the corporate bond origination business in London, our vision was to be the best corporate bond house as measured by our client relationships, quality of advice, and market share. Our strategy was to collaborate with our colleagues in corporate finance to target blue chip companies with whom the firm already had strong relationships and to offer superior advice based on our track record in other markets.

To make this happen, at the individual level, we needed to envision ourselves beyond our business unit silo and become the connecting bridge across multiple groups within the firm. We determined that we needed to go on an internal "road show" to share with each group the message about this new opportunity, what role each of us would play if we were to win, and why it was a good thing for each of them to embrace.

For most of us, even when we want to be visionary and strategic, there are many forces working against us. We're busy or in firefighting mode, which isn't conducive to thinking broadly about future trends and how we can take advantage of them. Our success to date has been based on knowing the detailed facts, being the technical expert, and getting things done—all of which use different "muscles" than vision and strategy. There's less immediate gratification from thinking and strategizing and more from finishing that report or closing the next deal.

Whatever your situation, it pays to start developing your vision and strategy Capability, because it becomes essential as we progress in our careers, whether in corporate, entrepreneurial, or non-profit circles.

> Having an inspiring vision and a credible strategy for achieving it attracts resources to your cause—people, financial, and other assets. This, in turn, increases your likelihood of success.

EVEN THE SMARTEST PEOPLE CAN MISS THE MOMENT

Gina graduated at the top of her class from a top university. She was the one who caught all the errors before the finished product went out the door—she loved to make things perfect. Her attention to detail was exceptional. So much so that she couldn't help but catch typos even when reading novels and newspapers—those early years of training were hard to shake.

Add to that her efficiency, pragmatic approach, and willingness to roll up her sleeves and "do the work." No wonder she was everyone's top choice to work on the most complex transactions. She was an amazing resource for the organization. Until she wasn't.

Looking back, Gina realized that there was a point in time when she kept doing the work on increasingly complex deals and prosecuting the business, but really shouldn't have. It was the point in time when others were starting to think more broadly, and lift their heads above the parapet to see the broader strategic themes, and learn to enter into those discussions with their colleagues and senior management.

What had seemed like unnecessary "blue sky" thinking and discussion to a do-er like Gina was actually her former peers demonstrating their ability to envision the future direction of the business, and pressure test their ideas. They were seen as leaders and given increasingly large parts of the business to run while Gina languished as a "safe pair of hands" in executing transactions.

Even more galling was the fact that Tony had been promoted ahead of her. They used to joke about Tony's lack of attention to detail and tendency to appear a little lazy, and wondered whether he would make it through the early years. But now, his big picture thinking and instinct for hanging back to reflect before diving into a project were paying dividends.

How could someone with Gina's abilities miss the forest for the trees? Gina wondered how she could recover, and why no one told her this was happening while it would have been easier to do something about it.

PUTTING VISION AND STRATEGY INTO PRACTICE

Having vision and being strategic will help you to contribute at a higher level and earn a seat at the leadership table. Here are four ways to hone your capabilities in this area:

1. **Understand the "space" in which your business operates and where you and your group fit in.** Do some thinking and reflecting on the big trends and themes in your sector, the 2-3 things that drive how successful your business can be, the other players who operate in the space, and the extent to which they are competitors versus potential partners. Is your market growing or shrinking? Becoming more complex or commodity-like?

Where do you see your organization or team fitting into that picture? Make sure you have a sense of the approximate scale and importance of your group relative to the overall organization.

2. **Start asking questions to generate insights into what you could do to move some of those levers and take advantage of trends.** For example:

What if we stopped doing A, B, and C? What if we had two times the funding? Ten times? What if the whole business went online? What would happen if we lost our biggest client? What would it take to become the best in the business? Double our margins? Serve a new client base?

3. **Take a more strategic approach to your current work.** You can demonstrate that you're strategic by showing you know what matters and what doesn't through the way you spend your time, energy, and attention. And that extends to the arguments you take on. Don't be one of those people who have to win every argument—whether it's about the fate of the company or which style of coffee maker to put in the kitchen.

At BP, they use the terms "Blue Chips vs. White Chips." In poker, the Blue Chips are worth a lot more than the White Chips, and it's important to identify when you're dealing with a Blue Chip issue. And let those White Chips go.

4. **Clear the decks so you have time to think and be strategic.** In order to be strategic, you need to clear some mind space and devote some mental energy to it. It's a different kind of rhythm from "getting things done" mode.

Carve out a block of time of at least two hours, and get your assistant to hold this time as sacrosanct. Go to a different room or place where you won't be disturbed. Give yourself a real chance to think.

That way, you can successfully oscillate between the big picture and the tasks required to make the big picture a reality.

PERSONAL ACTION PLAN FOR VISION AND STRATEGY

What are the three biggest themes that affect the future of my business sector and how are we positioned to take advantage of them?

How could I evolve my role into one where I can make a stronger contribution to the strategic direction of the business?

When people ask me about my business, how can I answer in a way that shows I am strategic?

Who could I talk to on a regular basis to help sharpen my strategic visioning capabilities?

What is the one thing I commit to do each month to be more strategic?

CHAPTER 5

DECISION MAKING: TAKING ACTION DESPITE UNCERTAINTY

According to the dictionary, a decision is "a conclusion or resolution reached after consideration," and decision making is "the thought process of selecting a logical choice from the available options."

Thinking, considering, and being logical are necessary but insufficient these days. You've then got to act.

That's why I prefer Arizona State University Professor Dan Brooks' definition of a decision: "An irrevocable allocation of resources."

Professor Brooks gives the example of saying, "I've decided to lose weight." In his view, that's at best a plan or an intention, and in many cases, a hope or fantasy! It's definitely not a decision. Until you pull the trigger on something, no value is created. That's why decision making must include action.

And there are two other aspects of decision making that are also important marks of an effective leader and manager.

The first is to be decisive—that is, to actually make the choice crisply and cleanly without falling into the "analysis paralysis" trap. Indecision puts the whole team on hold. No forward progress is possible. While wavering before making a tough decision is natural, give it a time limit and don't do it in public. It's the equivalent of watching your eye doctor hover over her instruments before choosing which one to bring up to your eye. It doesn't inspire confidence.

The second is to be able to decide and move on. Wavering once you've said "charge" slows down progress. When you have doubts, others around you become less committed as well and that can make a perfectly good plan fall to pieces for lack of consistent execution.

Whatever role you play in the organization, your decisiveness or lack thereof can make or break your success as you become more and more senior.

To quote American General George S. Patton, "A good plan violently executed now is better than a perfect plan executed next week."

This Capability is about making strong, decisive choices and then confidently moving ahead in spite of the increased uncertainty that's the new norm.

When it's your decision to make, you will come across as being decisive if you make the decision crisply, act on it, and move on. Get out of the habit of wavering, and commit to learning from your decisions instead.

WHY YOU MUST DECIDE AND MOVE ON

The message from my department head is clear: "May, you have to decide, then move on. Decide; move on." He repeats these last three words several more times, accompanied by hand movements for emphasis—a downward karate chop for "decide," and a sweeping motion to the right for "move on."

I'm now an officer of the firm, and my department head is giving me my year-end review. It turns out that I'm driving my team crazy. I can't seem to make up my mind on what materials I want in preparation for client meetings. I keep changing the directive even after the team has started working.

And on the bigger decisions, like who to bring to the meeting or what's the right advice for the client, once I finally make a decision, I am wracked with anxiety about whether it was the "right decision." The "what if ..." factory in my brain starts working overtime, and it falls to my team (all of whom are junior to me) to "talk me down" from the proverbial ledge and soothe me back into a clear state of mind where I can recall why I chose to do what I did.

This indecisiveness ultimately cost me at least a year in promotion time. It had nothing to do with ability and everything to do with fear, perfectionism, and lack of clarity—all of which are the enemies of making and acting on good decisions.

Flash back seven years to when I even struggled to choose what to order for dinner—something new or an old favorite? Was it too expensive? Was it worth the calories? Would I have "dinner envy" when I saw what others ordered? Then I'd finally order something ... only to run back to the kitchen and locate our waiter and ask to make a change. It became a joke among the group. How many times will May change her dinner order this time? I finally overcame this when a friend reminded me that, "You know, you are going to eat again," and I was able to frame it as a series of experiments over time and gave myself permission to "get it wrong." I taught myself to decide and move on and I've seen others get over their worry and perfectionism too.

Coming back to today, the fact that the world is so much more complex, volatile and uncertain presents both challenges and opportunities to us as decision-makers. On the one hand, this can make us doubt our decisions. On the other hand, this gives us more opportunities to make adjustments—essentially, new decisions—as things around us inevitably change. We continuously alter course, just like a sailboat tacks toward its desired destination under changing wind and wave conditions.

PUTTING DECISION MAKING INTO PRACTICE

Leaders are called on to make many decisions. Here are five ways to become a better decision-maker:

1. **Make fewer decisions**. As Barry Schwartz writes about in *The Power of Choice,* the human brain can only make so many decisions in a day before "decision fatigue" sets in. That's why it pays to routinize as many as you can so you preserve your decision making Capability for the important ones.

2. **Make decisions earlier in the day.** Based on the same research, the best time of day for decision making is in the morning before you've used up your quota. That's because decision making involves risk, which is challenging because of complexity and uncertainty. Dealing with all of this requires clarity of thought, which you're more likely to have earlier in the day.

3. **Frame decisions so they can be made.** Decisions can be hard to make and sometimes it comes down to the way they are framed. That is, the way they are presented, thought about, or looked at. This is particularly important when you are faced with an unpleasant tradeoff. In cases of such "either/or" decisions where neither option is attractive, challenge yourself to find a "third way"—one that takes the best of both alternatives and creates a new one that is superior.

   For example, we were asked to choose between two competing teams who both wanted to offer us a service— one more dependable but the other one more creative. We reframed the decision to focus on how best to achieve our bigger goal of having a creative solution we could count on. This led us to challenge the "either/or" assumption and to ultimately ask the two teams to work together to provide us with the best of both worlds.

4. **Have a decision making protocol.** Just as golfers have pre-shot routines, it's helpful to have pre-established ground rules for you and your team. For example, clarifying who makes which decisions, keeping abreast of what's at stake for various stakeholders, and having a protocol for whether, when, and how to consult others (or not). Figure out what works for you and create a routine.

5. **Let values underpin your decisions.** Our decisions are based on our values. That's why it's so important to know

what the values are at a variety of levels: your personal values, those of your team, and those of the organization. Embedded in every organization is a "touchstone"—the single objective that matters the most to the organization's success—that acts as a guiding principle in making difficult decisions. Sometimes it's clearly stated, other times you have to figure it out yourself. But it's worth figuring out, especially so that you can make sure you've joined an organization whose values align with your own.

PERSONAL ACTION PLAN FOR DECISION MAKING

What is the "touchstone" or guiding principle for my organization—the single most important objective that drives our success and that we can all rally around?

What are the personal principles and values that form my basis for decision making?

Who needs to see me act decisively and make good decisions?

When am I at my best in terms of decision making?

Which decisions can I "routinize"?

I commit to taking this one action every day to become a better decision-maker:

CHAPTER 6

CREATING NEW BUSINESS: TRANSITIONING FROM CARETAKER TO RAINMAKER

To get ahead in your chosen field, one of the most important things you must be able to do is deliver results. Results are not the equivalent of handing in your assignment on time and in excellent shape. That's necessary but insufficient these days.

Creating new business is about producing results and outcomes beyond what currently exists, in a way that is tied to what matters most to your organization. Have at least one eye (and better yet two!) firmly on the outcome that matters most to your organization so that you can grow your contribution to the business in the most powerful way.

You can do this whether you're in a revenue generating part of the organization or not, and the same concept applies to organizations that aren't about making money, such as non-profits, governmental agencies, and educational institutions.

For example, being commercial in a charity could look like figuring out how to serve more people with the same level of resources, or finding new potential donors to sustain the effort for the long term.

And if you're in a business area that is not directly revenue generating, being commercial could mean being astute in managing legal risk, cost efficiency, or innovation opportunities for the company.

I call this being a "rainmaker." Being someone who makes great things happen for the organization that can be seen, felt, or heard.

You also need to show you can do it in a way that in a way that renews the organization, expands its set of opportunities, and improves its prospects. Your rainmaker contribution works best when it creates opportunity and success for the whole organization. That's what I call "growing the pie."

By having a "rainmaker" rather than a "caretaker" mindset, you are more likely to be perceived as truly valuable at the next level and advance your career.

> A "caretaker" processes the assignments put in front of him to an excellent standard. A "rainmaker" identifies activities that can take the organization to the next level. Both are important, but the latter is necessary to advance beyond mid-level.

YOU CAN CHOOSE TO BE A RAINMAKER FROM ANY SEAT

Wendy was an in-house lawyer at a subsidiary of a Fortune 100 company. As part of the litigation team, she dealt with an increasing volume of lawsuits every year. Not only were the litigation costs rising, the reputational risk to the company was going up as well.

She could have gone about her business and focused on handling the lawsuits to the best of her ability. Instead, she started asking questions about whether these lawsuits could be prevented. She began to investigate the chain of events that led to these situations landing on her desk.

She discovered that many situations could have been nipped in the bud before they became litigation events if people in the business units were more aware of the implications of when to escalate issues internally and how to defuse situations through better handling of complaints.

She then developed an Early Warning System (EWS) to help do just that. Working with her counterparts in the business to roll out the process helped insure buy-in. This raised her profile as well. Most importantly, it saved the subsidiary millions and improved their image and customer relationships.

As a result, Wendy won the CEO's award for innovation, and was asked to roll out her EWS to all the other subsidiaries. The following year, she was promoted to head of litigation. She attributes this success to having created this new opportunity that added value to the business and organization.

PUTTING CREATING NEW BUSINESS INTO PRACTICE

Those who can expand the organization's set of opportunities are usually valued beyond all others. Here are four ways to hone your capability in this dimension:

1. **Identify the most important outcome(s) for your organization.** Think about what your organization must deliver in order to be successful. See if you can narrow this down to one or at most 2-3 key outcomes.

   In professional services, it could be to make money for the firm by serving clients in the best possible way. For educators, it might be turning out a certain number of well-prepared graduates. For researchers, it could be creating new knowledge and publishing it. For an investment firm, perhaps it's delivering superior returns and keeping costs down.

2. **Figure out how you and your group can contribute.**
   Using a machinery analogy, there are a certain number of
   levers an operator can pull to affect the output, and some
   are more powerful than others. The same goes for each of
   us in our own organizations.

   As a banker, my strongest lever for creating new business
   was to build client relationships. I could make the biggest
   difference through a combination of expanding our
   market share with existing clients and breaking into new
   client relationships.

   For my colleagues in the Controller function, it meant
   finding ways to streamline the process of providing the
   business units with real-time information so they could
   manage the business more accurately.   In the case of a
   friend working in an African charity, it was to uncover
   an entirely new way to attract donations from a different
   pool of potential donors.

3. **Create a safe space to test your ideas and practice.**
   Identify the network of people who can act as a confidential
   sounding board to help you "test drive" your idea(s).
   Perhaps you have trusted colleagues in your group who
   are particularly open-minded, creative, and commercial to
   bounce around ideas with you.

   It can also help to get input from people outside the group
   who have a broader perspective—and whose cooperation

you will need to move things forward. If there are no confidentiality issues, you may want to talk to external parties. These could range from potential customers to subject-matter experts to wise mentors.

4. **Learn from your network what will "move the needle" the most.** Approach people in batches so you always have several people to learn from on the horizon. Start with the most "user-friendly" or low risk and progress to more discerning audiences from there.

    Listen with an open mind rather than seek to defend your idea. Incorporate what you've learned and make it an iterative process. This helps strengthen your idea into one that will really move the needle. All while getting buy-in at the same time!

PERSONAL ACTION PLAN FOR CREATING NEW BUSINESS

What critical business outcome(s) must my organization deliver in order to thrive?

How can I (and my team) contribute most powerfully to those outcomes? What "levers" are at my disposal?

What specific actions I can take to grow the pie and create new business?

Who do I need to talk to in order to learn more and "test drive" my ideas?

I commit to take this one action each week in order to create new business:

WORKING ON YOUR SELF

You are the most valuable and portable asset you have, more so than the school you attended, the car you drive, or the money you have in the bank. Every investment you make in yourself is worthwhile because it travels with you no matter where you go and can be accessed immediately. You are unique and when you work on your Self, it enhances the impact you can make in the world.

Working on your Self involves understanding who you are and how to manage yourself so you can perform to your potential (**Self-Awareness**), showing up in a powerful and visible way so that you are seen, heard and respected (**Presence and Profile**), and forming a community of support around you so that you can accelerate your career as well as recover from inevitable setbacks (**Building Your Community**).

CHAPTER 7

SELF-AWARENESS: UNDERSTANDING AND MANAGING YOURSELF

Self-awareness is about knowing yourself and what makes you tick, and being able to manage yourself so that you can continue to learn and grow no matter what else is going on around you. Embedded in this is being grounded—knowing who you are and what you came here to do and not letting things get to you or push you off track.

To use a driving analogy, it means knowing what your vehicle is capable of, the care that's required to keep it in top condition, and equipping it with whatever is needed so that it's able to operate at the optimal level under whatever road conditions come your way.

Self-awareness and self-management will also help remove many of the self-induced obstacles that stand between you and greater success. It will help you to operate as your best self more of the time, and put yourself in a position to succeed. Being more self-aware and able to self-manage will also help you with all the other Achiever Capabilities.

Without self-awareness, you're at risk of falling way short of your potential and goals by accident and not by choice.

Knowing your tendencies, how you want to play into them, and which ones to change because they no longer serve you well can make or break your career, help you find the "right fit" as you move forward, and open new doors you hadn't even seen on your horizon.

> When you are self-aware, grounded, and able to self-manage, you become comfortable in your own skin. This is the ultimate form of confidence.

WHAT IT LOOKS LIKE

A client of mine (let's call her "Susan") was hired to help with large change management projects at a blue chip corporation. She had always been the upstart smart kid who came up with innovative approaches and got away with challenging the status quo successfully because of her youthful passion, dedication, and the fact that her heart was in the right place.

However, the company she had recently joined was far more conservative and hierarchical. Susan was more senior, yet they weren't taking her seriously.

Susan was frustrated that she hadn't been able to sell her ideas and couldn't understand why her new colleagues weren't "getting it." Worse yet, they would ask her questions she had considered but discarded three iterations prior to the final version she presented. Didn't they know how hard she worked to provide them with the best solution—one with a bow tied around it? It made her angry just to think about how ungrateful and stubborn they were being.

She elicited some feedback, and discovered she was coming across as a "know-it-all," pitching ideas that would never work. Not at all what she had expected to hear.

Reflecting on this and after much discussion, Susan concluded three things. First, she needed to manage her tendency to get defensive and argue when challenged. Instead, she would breathe, separate her "self" from the idea, mentally swivel around to their side of the table, and draw on one of the stock phrases we came up with, such as, "That's interesting. Tell me more about how that would work."

Second, she would leverage her special strength—the ability to envision a better way of doing things—but do it in a way where she could bring people along. That meant having conversations with others along the way to "co-invent" the solution rather than springing her full-blown conclusion on them at the end.

Finally, she realized that this group was not the most natural environment for her to shine, and that other parts of the organization would be a better long-term fit. However, working on these lessons would stand her in good stead in the meantime.

Once Susan implemented these changes and saw progress, her confidence grew, which in turn helped her be less defensive, more integrated into the group, and more effective in her role.

PUTTING IT INTO PRACTICE

Being self-aware and able to self-manage is a foundational Capability that enhances our performance in all other areas. Here are four steps to take in order to improve:

1. **Gather data.** No matter how self-aware we think we are, we all have blind spots. Often, those blind spots—both positive and negative—are what hold us back from achieving greater success and fulfilling our potential.

   The Johari Window is a tool for improving self-awareness, identifying blind spots, and enhancing mutual understanding between individuals (as well as groups). See how much you can broaden the top left "pane" of the Johari Window, which is where we are most productive, by getting feedback from those who know you well and who you trust.

JOHARI WINDOW

	I KNOW ABOUT MYSELF	I DON'T KNOW ABOUT MYSELF
THEY KNOW ABOUT ME	My open self	My blind spot
THEY DON'T KNOW ABOUT ME	My hidden self / Their blind spot	Unknown/Unknown

Some questions you could ask include: "What do you see as my best strengths in a work context?" "Relative to others at my level, what do you see as my standout strengths?" "In my role as _____, what should I start, stop, and keep doing?" "In the context of running the team meeting, what could I do to make the session more effective?"

2. **Reflect and notice.** Step back and look at the data dispassionately. Resist the temptation to either discard it all as irrelevant or accept it all as completely true. Remember, feedback is partly about you and partly about the giver. Choose 1-2 points to observe about yourself as you go through the day. For example, being defensive when others challenge you, or not speaking up in meetings. Once you start noticing certain behaviors and recognizing when they kick in, you can choose to change them.

3. **Devise experiments.** Take action by finding small experiments you can do to move into a new behavior. For example, introducing yourself to someone within 60 seconds of entering the room if you're shy. Conduct 2-3 experiments at a time to speed things along, and choose ones that don't "bet the farm." Test out what behaviors work best for you.

4. **Extract the lessons.** Keep track of what works well and learn from the failed experiments. In both cases, extract the lessons and move forward.

PERSONAL ACTION PLAN FOR SELF-AWARENESS

What are my best strengths—the things that I am great at and love doing? What sets me apart?

What is my best soil—the environments where I perform at my best and feel most on top of my game?

What are *my likely derailers* for the situations when I am most likely to go off track, what triggers them, how do I behave, and what are the implications?

What are my antidotes for those derailing behaviors? What can I replace them with instead?

What are the 2-3 ways I can leverage my strengths so I can be more effective and improve my prospects?

I commit to take this one action every day in order to become more self-aware and grounded:

CHAPTER 8

PRESENCE AND PROFILE: SHOWING UP AS YOUR BEST SELF AND BEING VISIBLE

No matter how competent you are in the technical aspects of your role, you'll have a hard time making your mark unless others notice, respect, and recommend you.

That's where presence and profile come into the picture. These are "two halves of a whole" related to how you are coming across.

Presence is how you show up when you're with other people. It's the way you carry yourself—how you present yourself in person to get people to take you seriously, and earn their confidence and respect.

Profile is about how visible you are to other people when you're *not* with them. Making sure your reputation is known more broadly beyond your immediate circle. At some point in your career, it's not who you know, it's who knows you. And ideally, they extol your virtues when you're not there, and think of you when an exciting new opportunity comes up.

Not everyone has both presence and profile to the same degree. You can have a lot of one and not a lot of the other. For example, an influential and award-winning academic can have a high profile, but lack presence in a meeting—not looking people in the eye, not being a strong public speaker, or not being someone who is comfortable with small talk.

On the other hand, a highly competent lawyer can have great personal presence—run a tough meeting with confidence, command a room, and look the part—yet lack profile if no one knows who she is outside of her own department and client project team.

If you're thinking that building your presence and profile are selfish pursuits that you can defer until later, stop right now!

It's not just about advancing your career. It's about doing what's good for the business.

When you show up in a way that commands respect, the word will spread. Then you're able to help more people and deliver bigger outcomes. And that has a positive ripple effect on everyone around you.

People will want to work on your team. You'll be able to choose the best partners for your projects because people will be coming to you with proposals. You'll be in a position to do more business because word-of-mouth will be working in your favor, and that benefits your team and organization.

It's a winning combination.

> Developing your presence and profile is not a selfish endeavor that's just about you. It's an essential Capability that benefits your team, your organization, your clients, and yes, even your family. Yet, the "how" of achieving the result rests squarely with you.

WHAT IT LOOKS LIKE

I could count on Ben to attend our group's morning meetings. However, he didn't "show up" in a way that gave him any oomph or presence. He would wander in sheepishly, holding a sheaf of papers, then sit in the far corner with his chair pushed away from the table. He had a quiet speaking voice and mumbled so it was hard to hear him from the other end of the room, and he didn't look me in the eye. Instead, he often played with a paper clip as he talked. He also had a tendency to preface his answers with tentative words like "Ummm, I'm not sure but … "

In contrast, Joan had a way of walking into the room with an air of confidence. The fact that she was tall and had great posture helped. She always sat at the table, alert and ready to participate. She had a neat moleskin notebook, her phone, and a pen with her. When I called on her, I could count on her to present her update in a clear, concise way and make it sound interesting and engaging. Beyond that, she seemed comfortable in her own skin and was even able to joke appropriately and get the group to laugh.

In other areas of the company that we dealt with, everyone knew Joan. When I went to client events in Joan's region, everyone knew her by reputation and respected her. Ben, on the other hand, seemed to be like those Olympic divers who make perfect dives—a clean entry into the water without making a ripple. While that's great for a career in competitive diving, it's not so good in careers outside of that sport.

PUTTING PRESENCE AND PROFILE INTO PRACTICE

In my experience, there are four main aspects that work together to deliver what we call "presence": Mindset, Verbal, Behavioral, and Physical.

MINDSET	VERBAL
• To what extent do you like and believe in yourself? • How do you want to "show up?" • To what extent do you feel aligned with your work environment?	• How do you speak (tone, speed, volume, clarity)? • How often and when do you speak (only if asked a direct question; beginning vs. middle vs. end of a meeting)?
BEHAVIORAL	**PHYSICAL**
• How do you sit? Stand? • How do you walk into a room? • What is your handshake like? • To what extent do you take up your space?	• How do you dress relative to others (clothes, shoes, accessories, hair, grooming)? • What is your default or "resting" facial expression (open, skeptical, angry, etc.)?

Figure out which area is most important for you to work on *right now*. It could be the area where there is the biggest gap between where you are and where you want to be. On the other hand, it could be the area that would give you most confidence if you were to address it. The most important thing is to choose one aspect and start.

Once you've addressed your presence, it's time to build a higher profile. Building up your profile involves working on both what you are known for and by whom.

In terms of what you are known for, your brand is what you want to convey and your reputation is what others actually perceive and experience. Since perception is reality, your reputation forms the basis for your profile.

To the extent there's a gap between your brand and reputation, you'll want to close it. Getting that alignment is the basis for developing a profile you'll be happy with.

One practical way to figure out the gap is to come up with the three words or phrases that you'd like to convey as your brand. Then, ask 3-5 people who know you well (and whose judgment you trust) for the three words or phrases that come to mind when they think of you professionally. The difference between your answer and theirs is the gap.

As for the audience with whom you need to have a high profile, a good place to start is with your Stakeholder Map from Chapter 1. These are the people who need to know who you are and what you bring.

PERSONAL ACTION PLAN FOR PRESENCE AND PROFILE

Which aspect of presence would most move the needle for me and why?

Who can I enlist to help me work on that aspect by helping me notice what I'm doing and giving me real-time feedback?

With which people and audiences would I most benefit from developing a higher profile?

What is the brand I want to convey vs. the reputation I currently have and what is the gap between them?

I commit to take this one action every week in order to build my presence and profile:

CHAPTER 9

BUILDING YOUR COMMUNITY: INVESTING IN YOUR NETWORK OF SUPPORTERS

It can be a cold hard world out there, and we all need to have people we can trust. People we can turn to. People who "have our back." People who rate us highly and recommend us. Our potential allies and alliances.

That trusted collection of people we're connected to is our *Community*. And unlike family, you can choose who is in your community as well as whose community you're a part of.

From a professional standpoint, these aren't necessarily your friends. They're the set of personal contacts, affiliations, and relationships you have. While you may know them to varying degrees, you can reach out to them for information, advice, support, and access to opportunities—and vice versa. They are distinct from your Stakeholders, who are people you must deal with, but who may or may not like, trust and respect you, and vice versa.

While everyone in your community is a Supporter, there are several roles within the community that are particularly valuable:

1. **Sponsor.** If you have someone advocating for you and looking out for your career, who is it? Relative to you, what area are they in, and is their star rising or falling? How much longer will that person be in a position to sponsor you? For example, if the person is nearing retirement or likely to be promoted to a different part of the organization, you may need to build relationships to find a new one soon.

2. **Mentors.** What are the most important areas in which you need mentors? Most of us benefit from having a few general career mentors and a larger number of mentors we can turn to for specific aspects of our personal and professional development such as navigating organizational politics, dealing with parenting challenges, managing a problem team member, and so forth.

3. **Peer Coaches.** These are people you are close enough to who can give you confidential feedback about behaviors you are seeking to change. For example, a colleague who

attends many meetings with you and can give you a signal when you are talking over a client. Or someone who can help you make sense of conflicts that pop up during the week.

4. **Connectors**. People who are well-connected with others within and outside the organization are an invaluable resource. They can make introductions for you when needed, and take pleasure in doing so.

5. **Raving Fans**. These are people who think you are wonderful and appreciate what you have done for them over the years. They speak well of you whenever they can and remind you of all the great things you've done. When you're down or feeling sorry for yourself, they can lift your spirits and remind you of what you are like as your best self.

> Your ability to succeed with greater speed and ease is directly related to the breadth, depth, and quality of the community you build.

WHAT IT LOOKS LIKE

I was introduced to Ted when he was in his mid-30s and looking for that "next right role." One that would get him back on a corporate track after the detour he took into arts management.

Coming from a musical family, Ted couldn't resist taking on the challenge of working on the turnaround of a performing arts center on the West Coast. He delivered on his part of the project quickly, and now he was chomping at the bit for his next challenge.

However, the management structure of the organization held limited opportunities in the near term. Unless his new boss moved on or something else changed, Ted was stuck in middle management for the foreseeable future.

Prior to this, Ted had had a strong start to his career. After graduating from the Air Force Academy and earning an MBA from Kellogg, he joined an aerospace firm where he was promoted rapidly. But now, with a young family to consider, Ted felt he needed to get his career back on an upward trajectory during these prime earning years.

Fortunately, Ted had kept in touch with colleagues and former mentors along the way. A coffee here, a call there, and helping a mentor's daughter with her application to the Academy a few years ago all turned out to be great investments in keeping his community fresh. Plus, being connected on LinkedIn made it easy to keep track of those supporters who were less frequent contacts.

Ted put together a game plan, reached out to his community, and was able to uncover multiple leads that put him well on his way to getting that "next right role."

In a time when more than 70% of jobs are found through connections and networking, Ted found that it pays off to make building your community a personal priority. It can be your safety net and support network when you're in times of need, and your accelerator when things are going strong.

PUTTING BUILDING YOUR COMMUNITY INTO PRACTICE

When it comes to building your community of supporters (and people you support), here are two ways to engage.

1. **Assess.** Take a strategic look at your current community to see whether you have a diverse mix of people. If you want to advance personally and professionally, it helps to have access to a strong network of supporters with complementary backgrounds.

   - **Is it as robust as you need it to be given your personal and professional aspirations?** They say we are the sum total of our six closest friends. If that's the case, then it matters a great deal who is in our community—who we are connected to and choose to spend time with. In my experience, it helps to have people in your community who are at least two levels more senior to your own.

   - **Where are the gaps, if any?**

   - **Is there a particular category in which would you like to build more relationships?** Sponsor, Mentor, Peer Coaches, Connectors, Raving Fans?

- **Who might you target and why?**

2. **Engage.**

   - **Say yes.** Make it a habit to say yes when opportunities come up to get together with people who are current or prospective members of your community. As with any relationship, repeated rejections erode the connection, and these connections are vital to your future success.

   - **Show up.** When the date you said yes to rolls around, make it a priority to show up. And when you show up, show up as your best self. The one that's positive and appropriate for the occasion.

   - **Keep in touch.** Find ways to maintain the connection that you can build into your normal days and weeks. It's okay to get help from your assistant (if you have one) to remind you. Send an article they might benefit from, or mail a birthday card. Just figure out a system that works for you and make it into a habit.

   - **Give and get.** It's not about keeping score, but it is important to have some degree of equality in the "balance of payments" between what each of you gives versus gets. Neither of you will want to always be the one asking or providing.

PERSONAL ACTION PLAN
FOR BUILDING YOUR COMMUNITY

Who are the 2-3 people I count on for advice right now, and what role do they play in my community (sponsor, mentor, peer coach, connector, raving fan, or simply a supporter)?

Which 1-2 people would I want to add to my community over the next 3-6 months and what roles would we play for each other?

What 1-2 ways of keeping in touch with my community could I work into my normal routine without it becoming a burden?

Which person in my community could I call on to help me accelerate my career right now and what would I ask of them?

I commit to take this one action every week in order to build my community:

CONCLUSION

MOVE THE NEEDLE: YOUR PERSONAL ACTION PLAN

Now that you've had the chance to do a deeper dive and "play" with one or two Capabilities, it's time to reflect on the themes and takeaways, bring it back up to a strategic level, and tie it into the broader context of your overall career goals.

There are many ways to synthesize and pull together what you've learned from going through this book—making a list, journaling, taping a post-it with a few key concepts to your computer or a place you'll see every day, creating a visual, and so forth.

The exact format is not so critical. What matters is that you give yourself the chance to think about how that Capability fits in, how it will move the needle for you, and what life will be like once you achieve the result you want or address an obstacle that's been holding you back.

I find it's helpful to write down my "why" and my "picture of success" for those times when I need encouragement to keep going. Sometimes that reminder is all it takes to shift the energy from feeling like it's "hard work" to something positive and full of ease.

For example, on the following page you will find a format you could use—it can fit on a 4" x 6" index card.

MY SUMMARY TAKEAWAYS AND PERSONAL ACTION PLAN

Arriving – This is my definition of success for my career:

Capability – This is the Capability that will most move the needle if I master it now:

Action – The action I commit to taking to master this Capability is:

Anticipating – Here are 1-2 possible obstacles that could come up and ways I can avoid or address them so they don't stop me from mastering the Capability:

Another approach I use in my workshops is to ask people to create a visual—one that conveys what they commit to do to move from where they are now to where they want to be on their chosen Capability.

Here's what one woman did at the end of a workshop I ran as a group activity. It's a visual representation of where she and the others in her group are on their Achiever Paths.

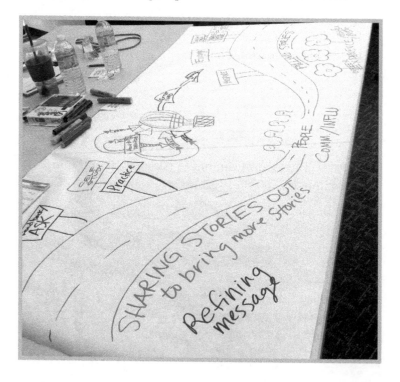

By now, we've covered lots of ground and, if you've followed along with this book, you will have made great progress on the three tasks ahead of you on the Achiever Path:

1. **Develop your Capabilities**. You've worked on the 1-2 Capabilities would most move the needle for your career and identified at least one action step that you are prepared to commit to.

2. **Own your own development**. You're clear on where you are and what "arriving" or success means for you.

3. **Be prepared for big and small milestones**. You're on the lookout for that "right mix" of Capabilities that will help you advance from where you are to the next step, and for the moments when you can show you have those Capabilities.

Remember that you are not alone in your career journey. Far from it. You're simply in a time of unprecedented uncertainty, volatility, and speed of change where one size doesn't fit all.

However, with the framework and strategies in this book, you now have support as you develop your own Achiever Path: the "What, Where, When, and How" of advancing your career so you can fulfill your potential and make the difference you were meant to make.

I look forward to continuing to support you in whatever way I can, and wish you every success in your career. And I want you to have fun in the process!

Above all, just keep going. The world is looking forward to seeing you be better, do more, and make the difference you are meant to make.

FURTHER RESOURCES

Resources to learn more and work on specific Capabilities in greater depth:

www.theacceleratebook.com/welcome

Ideas, Insights & Inspiration on Career Success and Leadership:

www.maybusch.com/blog

Individual Coaching, Consulting and Speaking:

www.maybusch.com/services

ABOUT THE AUTHOR

May Busch faced a wide range of challenges during her 24-year career in investment banking. From hiring the wrong people to be being shifted out of jobs and passed over for promotions, she experienced just about every pitfall, setback and misfortune the corporate world can dish out. However, those mistakes empowered May to learn what it takes to succeed in a changing workplace, achieving her goal of becoming a Managing Director and, ultimately, Morgan Stanley's Chief Operating Officer for Europe. Now, she is using the hard lessons she learned to help other achievers take ownership of their careers and enjoy a faster, smoother climb to success.

Through her international consulting practice based in the U.K., May Busch & Associates Ltd, May works with senior management of corporations and professional services firms on organizational strategy, leadership development, and client effectiveness. She offers workshops, keynotes, consulting and executive coaching to high-potential and high-performance leaders and their teams, focusing on bringing her insights and experiences to help them advance their organizations and to promote greater thought leadership, diversity and entrepreneurial spirit in the workplace.

May also serves as a Senior Advisor in the Office of the President and Professor of Practice at W.P. Carey School of Business at Arizona State University, and has lectured at Imperial College Business School, Cass Business School, Stanford University's Clayman Institute for Gender Research, and Harvard University's Office of Career Services. She holds a BA magna cum laude in Economics from Harvard University, an MBA from Harvard Business School and is a graduate of The Meyler Campbell Business Coach Programme. She is married and has three children. *Accelerate* is her first book.

INDEX

A
achiever capabilities. *See* capabilities
achiever paths
    defined, 4
    progressing along, 102–103
advancement
    and building your community, 84, 95
    and capabilities, 5, 7, 15, 17, 103
    and the need for team leadership, 31–33
    and the rainmaker mindset, 66–67
Angelou, Maya, 41
audiences, 40, 43–44, 46, 88, 89

B
bad bosses, 36
behavioral presence, 86–87
Ben (example) on presence & profile, 85–86
Brooks, Dan, 57–58
building your community
    defined, 6, 17, 91–92
    example, 93–95

G

I

J

L

M

N

O

P

T

U

V

Lightning Source UK Ltd.
Milton Keynes UK
UKHW021854160220
358811UK00005B/787

9 780993 545108